Debt Free College –
We Did It!

(The God Factor in Avoiding Student Loans)

By Lynn Lusby Pratt

PRESS

Xulon Press
www.xulonpress.com

To order additional copies, call 1-866-909-BOOK (2665).

Dedication...

To Karis who led the way,
blazing a clear trail of faith and courage
for the kid brothers and cousins.

Table of Contents

Chapter 1 — Introduction

"Of course it won't work. That's the fun of it!"

Our daughter has completed three years of college and plans to graduate. There have been no student loans. No, she did not qualify for a full ride. We aren't paying her way. Nor is she working ridiculous hours. And although an extreme financial crisis made us the most "for sure" student loan candidates around, we firmly refused to take that route.

That was the first paragraph in my article, "Lord of Financial Aid," which appeared in *The Lookout* June 11, 1995. Some readers were skeptical. Perhaps a lucky break or two had made it possible for our oldest child to manage her first three years of college without taking loans. But how would the scenario play out as time went on and as the kid brothers entered the picture?

Since that article was published, Karis has graduated debt free (five years of school). Her younger brother Cason graduated as I'm writing this—also debt free (five years). The youngest, Clinton, has finished his third year. Debt free. (He will graduate in two more years.)

Their cousin Arian has just completed her second year of college. Same plan. Same results.

That's 15 years of college. Debt free.

What follows are the particulars of how they did it.

I won't say we didn't think about loans when Karis started the college application process. We did. Loans were the hot topic at financial aid meetings sponsored by the high school guidance department. Some families considering loans were obviously frugal people of modest means. Their rationale was much like mine: *My child has put up with used prom clothes, sack lunches, and bicycles instead of cars. I can't bear the final insult—her missing the first year of college with her peers.*

I knew just how they felt.

Other loan applicants were three-car families who ate out several times a week and ordered $40 underwear from shops with names like Lamarr's of L.A. and Drusilla's Drawers. Loans seemed to be the answer for everyone.

At these financial aid meetings, parents good-naturedly made light of their children's impending debt: "At least Becky will learn the meaning of $10,000. Plus interest." As they chuckled, I found it hard to join in. I envisioned large numbers of young people (some wearing expensive underwear) beginning their adult lives financially crippled.

Few seemed worried, however. Even now, the student loan business continues to boom. Indeed, six years after Karis started college, her brother Clinton attended the financial aid session during freshman orientation week at college, where it was assumed every college freshman was applying for loans. Forms were automatically distributed.

Clinton raised his hand. "Do we have to fill this out if we're not getting loans?" he asked.

Everyone turned and stared.

Even the instructor stared.

Since Clinton had an older brother and sister attending college without loans, he had assumed that at least *some* other students were doing the same. So he was surprised to find himself odd man out. Though it was an awkward moment, Clinton wasn't embarrassed. Rather, he was concerned about his classmates and what they might be letting themselves in for by going into debt. With our family's ongoing interest in the topic of student loans, he knew some of the facts:

- In 1997, college graduates had an average debt of $18,000.[1]
- To pay this back, a graduate needs to earn $38,000 a year.[2]
- Actual average income upon graduation is only about $24,000.[3]
- There used to be a ten-year limit on repaying student loans. But now there are many options offering a thirty-year plan. So, for example, a Stafford Loan of $17,200 at 8.25% interest over 30 years will cost $46,440.[4] Double this amount if the person you're marrying is in the same boat.

Imagine yourself a newlywed facing almost $100,000 of debt—and you haven't even bought a house!

- Banks are willing to give students incredible amounts in the form of student loans— $100,000 maximum.[5]
- In addition, the average college student is carrying a $2200 credit card balance.[6]
- Since 1980, defaulted college loans have cost taxpayers over 20 billion dollars.[7]

Clearly, things are out of control. The students in Clinton's financial aid session looked at him as if he were crazy. But *I'm* looking at *them!*

"No!" I want to scream at these smart and promising, but penniless, young people. "Don't do it!"

> *"Better a little with the fear of the Lord than great wealth with turmoil." —Proverbs 15:16*

"Yes!" say many legislators, who favor passing laws that would enable every young person in America to qualify for student loans.

"No!" financial experts say. "Get out of debt and stay out."

"Yes!" say college representatives. "It's an investment in your future."

What to do? Whose advice to take?

Listen. No matter where you buy your underwear, you *can* avoid the student loan route by claiming this simple policy:

"Putting my trust in the Lord of Financial Aid, I *will not* go into debt for college."

Hey, I heard that groan. And I know the protests by heart: "That's simply not being realistic. Why, even if God provided half…that's still…let's see…well, it just won't work."

Of course it won't. That's the fun of it! It's exactly the sort of thing God specializes in. Have we forgotten that God promises he will provide what we need?

> He " …is able to do immeasurably more than all we ask
> or imagine." —Ephesians 3:20

Financial guru Dave Ramsey says, "There is not one place in the Bible where it says it is OK to borrow money. There is not one place where God used debt as a tool to help or save His people."[8]

As financial consultant Larry Burkett tells parents, "Remember that college loans, like any loans, restrict God's ability to direct us. What if God has an alternate plan for financing your children's college educations, but you don't ever explore it because of readily available loans?"[9] To use an analogy from the Bible story of Abraham and Isaac, we place our students on the sacrificial altar of student loans, raise the knife and never even look to see if there's a lamb in the bushes!

I fretted and wrung my hands about my children's financial future.

> "Do not fret—it leads only to evil." —Psalm 37:8

Then I claimed the above prayer policy—"Putting my trust in the Lord of Financial Aid, I *will not* go into debt for college"—as my own.

How can you actually put the policy into practice? I'm confident our experience will give you guidelines and save you a bucket of trouble.

[I need to say here, for the benefit of any atheists who may have picked up this book: It is possible to graduate from college without debt even if you don't believe in God. Now, I certainly don't recommend that. For one thing, it will be a very dull ride. You'll miss all the fun, all the miracles. But the fact is, it is impossible for anyone—believer or not—to go into debt if he doesn't apply for any loans. Stay with me a little longer.]

The key to remaining debt free is to make the statement *"I will not apply for any loans"* the one college factor from which you won't budge.

Instead, most students have other factors from which they won't budge. For instance:

"I must start college this fall."

"I must attend Such-and-Such University."

"I must graduate in four years."

And so forth. Other, lesser have-tos also factor in:

"I have to have a car."

"I have to get my own apartment."

"I have to buy a cell phone."

Naturally, if you insist on starting school this fall but fail to have the money required by the due date, there is no alternative but to take a loan.

Or, say your goal is to do whatever it takes to graduate in four years. If the homework load is too heavy for you to manage having a job, you give in and take a loan.

But, if you commit to not applying for loans, you will start adjusting other things to fit that decision. For instance, you may choose a different school; you may work a semester first; you may sell your car; you may attend school part-time....

We determined that we were not going into debt, nor were we signing up our children to go into debt. They didn't have any idea what kind of burden that would be. But *we* did.

Only a few years earlier we had returned from the Japan mission field with no home, no car, no possessions and no job. I remember that, in my weaker moments, I was jealous of the Cambodian refugees featured in the news at the time. ("At least *they* own a couple of pots!") My father helped us with small promises-to-pay so we could buy a car, as well as food and clothing. I'm grateful. But I'm not absolutely sure we did the right thing financially. At the time I saw no other route to take. But maybe the Lord would have provided in another way, if we hadn't been afraid of waiting till the last minute. I understand the feeling of panic in such circumstances.

The next few years were excruciating. Even at this point in the story, when Karis was ready to enroll in college, we were still struggling and were very, very careful with money.

Naturally, given this history, we didn't want the children to endure needless suffering. But our plan to avoid student loans appeared to be financially impossible.

Friends scoffed at the idea of no loans.

But the Lord says, "Those who hope in me will not be disappointed." —Isaiah 49:23

Starting with Karis, we simply moved forward, making decisions that seemed best. In other words, we based our decisions on what we believed was the right thing to do, not on fears about money (or the lack thereof). We decided to press on until the doors to the halls of learning slammed in our faces.

But they never did.

"Your Father knows what you need before you ask him." — Matthew 6:8

This is not to say that it is God's plan for every student to attend college, start school this fall, continue uninterrupted until graduation, etc. But I do believe God blesses us when we seriously commit to his principles. Basically, the principles we were trying to live by—in other areas of our lives as well as in the college finance situation—are outlined in this Scripture:

"But seek first his kingdom and his righteousness, and all these things will be given to you as well." —Matthew 6:33

• *Put God first.*

To us, putting God first financially meant giving God at least 10% of our income. Off the top. The Bible calls this 10% given to

God a "tithe." While I believe the Bible indicates that 10% is a good starting amount, I'm not going to argue that in this book. People who are new to the idea may certainly start by giving God whatever they want—even if it's less than 10%.

"If you want to give, your gift will be accepted."
—2 Corinthians 8:12, New Century Version

At the same time, my use of the term "tithe" or "God Money" is not limited to 10%. More is better. Both terms are used rather loosely throughout this book, meaning simply the amount the giver has designated for God.

- *Go after his righteousness...imitate his "right"-ness.*

Doing what's right financially meant we paid our bills on time, even when the math said it wouldn't work. And we were honest in all financial matters.

- *He will provide.*

We lived on what was left, trusting him to provide. Matthew 6:33 is God's promise to feed and clothe us if we put him first and do what's right. We believed him.

These are the students' individual accounts, written from their status as of summer 2000. The details are different: good grades, average grades; savings account, no savings account.... But the principles are the same.

Before you read on, I must impress upon you to lay aside your calculators. The math is truly puzzling. It will appear that some important data has been left out; or perhaps there are typographical errors. An engineer friend of mine once said, "There are no miracles in mathematics." But he didn't understand The God Factor. So, be forewarned: The God Factor plays happy havoc with figures!

As proof, I offer the Bible's account of the feeding of the 5,000 (John 6:1-13). Conventional math would project that equation as:

5,000 lunches needed - 1 lunch in hand = 4,999 lunches needed

At least, that's how it looks without The God Factor. WITH The God Factor, the actual problem worked out like this:

1 lunch x The God Factor = 5,000 lunches + 12 baskets of leftovers

This equation would never appear in a math book. It's unbelievable. But it IS correct.

That's the point. When The God Factor is involved, a calculator can only do so much.

Chapter 2 — Karis's Story

"Why did everybody but me get a Pell Grant?"

Karis was a top student and in line for several scholarships. Having been employed off and on throughout high school (tutoring, babysitting, working at the public library), she had a fair-sized savings account. She also had won a piano competition scholarship at Cincinnati Bible College. So we were taking the steps for her to enroll there.

Still, you have to understand how little we had, how foolish it was for us to think Karis could go to college without loans....

It was only five years earlier that we had had nothing but a suitcase. We were now living in a cheap eighty-year-old house, had only one car, rarely ate out, did laundry every few days to have enough clothes. A garage sale to raise money was out of the question—we didn't have a garage! There was no shed, no attic, nothing in the basement; and the four small closets had plenty of extra space.

Luckily—or so I thought—we would receive sympathy and help by filling out the "special circumstances" section of the FAFSA form (Free Application for Federal Student Aid). I spent hours condensing our sad story into a compelling paragraph.

When the results came back, I was horrified. Our needs had been ignored. And our form had obviously been confused with the royal family's—we were placed in a category that simply wasn't fair. To the FAFSA people, we appeared well off, because we had no big debts and last year's salary had been good. In a sense, we *were* well off: We didn't have a second mortgage, three car payments, or wallets full of maxed out credit cards. The tiny amount of cash we had in the checking account was actually a possession of ours. We were in the black, so to speak. But we had been scrimping for years to keep our heads above water, and I wanted someone to understand. I wanted cash! The FAFSA people, however, weren't interested in our history.

On the other hand, our friends who showed well in public with their new houses, three cars, and luxury vacations, appeared poorer on the FAFSA application, because they actually did have less. Their tiny amount in the checking account disappeared in the face of thousands and thousands of dollars of debt for all those possessions.

I considered our friends poor managers. But the FAFSA people called them needy. My own exasperation would later be echoed in an article titled, "My Kid's College Fund Blues."[10] As writer Blake Hurst explained, working and saving for college often appear to go against the student. It's enough to make a person quit trying. Hurst vented his frustration, but was unable to offer any satisfying countermeasures. I understood his pain. But the person who believes in the Lord must take heart—and take a different view. When we do what pleases the Lord, he makes things right—no matter how disturbing the immediate situation is. But he does it in his own way and in his own time.

Several bubbles burst with our FAFSA results. Proud of the paragraph I'd written, I had entertained a fantasy in which a benevolent billionaire read of our plight and offered to pay our daughter's way through school—possibly even throwing in a handsome clothing allowance and a red convertible!

I cried all day over these first reports.

Looking back, the mistake I made is obvious: I had put my faith in the FAFSA people. And when they didn't come through, I crumbled. But the FAFSA people aren't in charge of the world. I'd forgotten that. I'd forgotten that my Lord is the Lord of Financial Aid.

"Is there any God besides me? No, there is no other Rock;
I know not one." —Isaiah 44:8

Just because the FAFSA people determine that parents should pay a certain amount doesn't mean it must go that way. There is no FAFSA sheriff. We needed only to push forward and trust God. And that's what we did—as soon as the shock of not receiving the red convertible wore off.

My memory of those days is that the entire family was in a state of perpetual nail biting and tears. It certainly was true of me. And, undoubtedly, my worried behavior boiled over onto Karis's dad.

This was our first experience with college applications, the FAFSA, scholarship forms…. We'd all had such tight financial belts for so long, I wanted our money situation to be improving. Instead, I saw more dire circumstances in our future.

But recently, as I interviewed Karis about that era, I was amazed to discover that her thinking had been on a completely different plane—a better one, I might add.

Though she expected to be totally on her own for college expenses (that is, without help from us), Karis saw herself as being in a better position than her friends were. She'd been managing her money well since junior high, so she had more money than her friends. She felt sure her good grades would net some scholarship money. She was not concerned about what would happen if she had to interrupt her college career by dropping out to work.

In addition, Karis had been disappointed that so many of her classmates' interests were trivial, revolving around hair styles and parties. She was excited about entering the Cincinnati Bible College environment. Campus visits had indicated that students there had the depth she wanted to explore.

All these factors had overridden any anxiety about finances. I was stuck in the moment. But Karis was moving forward.

Speaking about King Hezekiah: "In everything that he undertook…he sought his God and worked wholeheartedly. And so he prospered." —2 Chronicles 31:21

We determined to give Karis our "parent contribution" weekly, like an allowance. During senior year in high school, her allowance had been $4 a week—at a time when some elementary students received $10 a week! We agreed to deposit $35 a week in her account. It seemed a reasonable amount for the situation—even though we didn't have it. I can't explain where that money came from. (I can't explain where lunch for 5,000 came from, either.) But, somehow, every payday it was there. This approximately $1800 a year was our only promised contribution for college.

To clarify: By high school graduation, our children knew they were responsible for their own money management, grades, work habits. They also knew we could not hand them a college education. In college, each of our students had his own checking account, containing all his own money and our weekly deposits. They were responsible for managing that account and paying ALL their expenses/bills from it. They were aware there wasn't any money lying around home. Even the usual places for finding extra change—under sofa cushions, in the laundry room, on the floor of the car—were clean at our house! We missed out on the experience of our college students "calling home for money," which so many parents joke about. Our kids' money calls were to tell us their status or ask for advice.

At the time, Cincinnati Bible College had no monthly payment plan; the entire first semester bill had to be paid up front. I had been concerned about this for months. But Karis did receive several academic scholarships. With her savings and graduation gift money, she had the semester payment when the time came.

After the first few days of college classes, Karis called home:

"Mom, everybody but me got a Pell Grant."

Karis hadn't thought any more about being refused a need-based Pell Grant (courtesy of the FAFSA evaluation) until she saw the circumstances of the students who were awarded one.

"These kids have cars," she complained, "and CD players, furniture, designer clothes, they eat out and go to the movies...." All of Karis's belongings had fit easily into our compact car.

Karis felt so wronged that she made an appointment with the school's financial aid lady. "Why do the people who have wasted their money get help and the careful, deserving people don't?" Karis asked bluntly.

The financial aid lady agreed that it seemed unfair—perhaps even *was* unfair. But in the long run, she said, we'd be better off. The spending habits of those other people would eventually backfire.

On some level, Karis felt better; and we knew the financial aid lady was right. Still, it would have been nicer if she'd said, "You poor dear. I'll have $20,000 transferred immediately into your account." Then Karis's needs would have been met, and we could have breathed a little easier. If we could fast forward here we'd see that Karis's needs *were* met—not on someone's order or in one lump sum, but step by step. The times we couldn't breathe easy were our own fault. We felt smothered whenever we forgot that the Lord of Financial Aid was in control.

Karis continued to live Matthew 6:33. When a bill was due, the money was there. She was in a school singing group which paid a tuition grant. She worked for a while in the school cafeteria. With no car and a very full schedule, working off campus would have been difficult. Even though the school cafeteria job paid minimum wage, it was handy, could fit into her schedule and had no expenses attached to it, such as transportation, uniform, etc.

This may sound like a lot of work and no fun. But Karis enjoyed many stress-relieving activities, including intramural and sand volleyball, Rich Mullins concerts, the $1.50 movie theater, playing euchre at Skyline Chili and a trip to Florida. One time she even …well …uh, as a mother I probably shouldn't tell you about Pittsburgh. See, she and a friend were talking one night. Karis said, "Hey, let's really go somewhere." The friend replied, "You mean like …PITTSBURGH?" And Karis said, "Yeah!" So they drove all night to Pittsburgh and back and had a terrific time. She had her footloose and fancy-free moments.

Karis bought things she REALLY needed or REALLY wanted, but she was careful. The Lord of Financial Aid increased her income: A faculty member recommended her for a small scholarship she didn't even know existed—and she got it. A music composition of hers won a contest that unexpectedly came with a scholarship. And a friend of the family presented her with a surprise gift of $1000.

"My God will meet all your needs according to his glorious riches in Christ Jesus." —Philippians 4:19

For clothes, Karis had always taken a dim view of hand-me-downs and throw-ups. (Throw-ups are what you call hand-me-downs you inherit from someone younger.) But in college she once said, to a girl whose clothing she admired, "I love your slacks." "Thanks," the girl smiled back, "they're my grandpa's." That incident tweaked Karis's thinking to: If it works, who cares where it came from?

In her junior year, Karis knew the Lord wanted her to spend the following year doing mission work in Japan where she had grown up as a missionary kid. It would be sad to miss graduating with her class. And scary going to Japan alone. Finances, though, posed the biggest problem. By the end of this third year, Karis's bank account would dwindle to zero. Since everybody knows mission work rarely provides high salaries, how would she ever be able to finish school the next year?

"'I know the plans I have for you,' declares the Lord, 'plans to prosper you and not to harm you, plans to give you hope and a future.'" —Jeremiah 29:11

Putting what was right ahead of money worries, she told the Lord she would go—even though she was not looking forward to raising support. But, having said YES to God, she discovered that he had arranged for more than she'd need—without raising support: A mission bought her $1000 ticket and gave her a $1000-a-month allowance; friends in Japan offered her use of a rent-free apartment (worth $500 a month); and a missionary signed her up to teach a few paying English classes. All of this help came unsolicited.

A couple of months before her year in Tokyo ended, she called home.

"Mom, I don't know what to do."

"What's wrong?"

"I have too much money."

I laughed. "What do you mean?"

"I just keep making money, and I can't get rid of it. If I put $50 in the offering, someone gives me $100. If I put $100 in, somebody gives me $200."

After a year of mission work in the most expensive city in the world, she had thousands of dollars.

"Good heavens!"

"Yeah."

"Well, the Lord knows you use it wisely. You must be supposed to have it."

In a final attempt to outdo the Lord's generosity, she flung a $1000 gratitude offering at Japan and returned home from the mission field—loaded. She was able to pay cash for her first car, had money for school, an apartment...and "12 baskets of leftovers."

The Lord says, "They will be in awe and will tremble at the abundant prosperity and peace I provide . . . ." —Jeremiah 33:9

At some point Karis had realized she would need an extra year to graduate. She was in a demanding music program and working, as well. So, with the year off for Japan, it would total six years between high school graduation and college graduation. But in a letter home, she wrote, "I'm less and less disturbed by the fact that I will not graduate until 1997. Hey, who really cares? What's important is my growth and maturity level, and that God's timing prevails."

As graduation time approached, Karis noticed a strange phenomenon among her classmates. They had studied for years to reach this moment, but many weren't excited about graduating. They were in debt. One friend owed over $10,000; at commencement one of the student speakers would mention a debt of over

$20,000. Such students were dreading graduation, because it meant they'd have to start repaying their loans. Some were contemplating going further into debt—entering graduate school in order to postpone repaying the loans. Others considered taking high-paying, boring jobs outside their field of study to pay off the loans.

Karis had none of these problems. She was a happy homecoming queen, excited about graduation. Karis was free.

The summer after graduation, Karis took a babysitting job. Though difficult in its own way, it was a much-needed change from study, enabling her to enjoy the summer sun at the pool. Over the next couple of years, she was active in music but largely not employed in the music field. She worked at various jobs through a temp agency and traveled extensively. Three years after graduation she is employed as a music editor in Seattle Washington, sings with a professional jazz group, teaches junior high Sunday school, and is planning a trip to Europe.

IN KARIS'S OWN WORDS: **In my high school days, boy, did I want a car, stereo system, trendy clothes, and all that jazz! But I was well aware of the cost of college, and definitely wanted to go. So I practiced self-control and even chose a job over sports for the last two years of high school.**

I also knew I could win the favor of my peers if I made lower grades so as not to "ruin the curve;" but I couldn't give up my self-respect or the opportunity for scholarships. By the time I graduated from high school, I'd saved quite a bit of money and was proud of it. Yet I was struck by what a small percentage of the total cost of college it represented. Even with my best efforts, I came up WAY short.

That's where The God Factor comes in. While I did my best to save my money and acquire scholarships, I had to practice being a good steward and obedient to the Lord. Faithfully tithing, following Christ and striving to be who he made us to be—those are the things that please him. And, I had to trust him that he would get me through college without loans, if that was where I was supposed to be. He promises to provide all we need to carry out his plan—and more! My college experience has proven this. God's way sure beats any other form of "financial aid."

Chapter 3 — Cason's Story

"Plant your money in a God pot and watch it grow!"

Perhaps some of you will better relate to Cason's story: Cason didn't have much savings money. During high school he *worked*—having been on the school sports teams, in the band, and a school office helper—but had rarely been *employed*.

He was an average student. Cason's report card tended to read:

Class	Grade	Teacher Comments
Chemistry	B-	Pleasure to have in class
Band	A	Pleasure to have in class
History	D+	Pleasure to have in class

He received a one-time local scholarship of $1000. That was it. Still, following Karis's lead, he started down the no-loan road, on his way to a telecommunications degree in video production.

Ohio University offered a monthly payment plan, which helped.

Strictly speaking, a monthly payment plan is a loan. OU added a flat $45 fee to the year's cost and spread the total out into nine payments. The student received a monthly bill for a set amount. This is a very short-term "loan." And there is no option—such as there would be with credit cards—to push payments forward by making only a "minimum payment;" and so, no danger of falling behind. Cason was also awarded a work-study job.

Before Cason moved into his dorm, he and his roommates assessed their possessions via phone. The roommates had TV, carpet, chair, CD player, phone, computer…. Cason had only Papa's bookcase—and a feather duster to keep everyone else's stuff clean!

But, in the festive spirit of leaving home, he was not embarrassed. The friends were even excited for his contribution to the room: "A duster? Yeah, we'll need that!"

This was going to be fun.

However, when he actually settled in to college life, he had a rude awakening: His friends weren't working, they had stuff, money to eat out and go to the movies. They felt sorry for poor Cason.

"You gotta *work*, man? Bummer."

Then *he* began to feel sorry for himself—and called home. After explaining these circumstances, he said, "This is gonna be hard. And I kinda don't see what the big deal is about the loans."

I outlined the situation as I saw it:

"Cason, the money your friends are spending isn't real. A loan paid their school bills. They have to pay that back. Since their bills are 'paid' for now, they feel like the money in their pockets is mad money.

"You're in a different position. You personally wrote a check for your school bill this month. You saw your balance drop. So you are very aware of your actual financial status.

"For example, you know that your check for the school payment includes the meal ticket; so $7 of that check paid for today's lunch in the school cafeteria. And you know if you just chuck that to go out for a $10 pizza... well, that would total $17 for today's lunch. Your job is paying you $22 today. You would be blowing most of today's salary on one meal. If you did this you'd be completely aware of what it all means. But your friends don't get it. They're just going, 'Hey, let's eat out today.' They have money in their pockets and a false sense of security that their bills are paid.

"If you can trust us and go with the plan for this one year, and see what you think when the year is up...."

He stuck with it.

Without using The God Factor, I cannot explain how he made it. The price tag for one year was $10,000. Here's his income list for the year:

Savings $500
Scholarship 1000
Graduation gifts 1500
Summer job 2000
Our contribution .... 2000 (we had raised our part to
$40 per week)
Work-study job 1750
8750

That looks close. But close is still not enough. And you know all the unexpected expenses that come up in addition.

All I can tell you is he continued to tithe, and didn't buy many extras. Though he did a fair share of fun stuff, most of his entertainment was free campus activities: school sports events, theatrical productions, video game parties in the dorm, intramurals....

Toward the end of the year, when students were signing up for the next year's classes, Cason called me:

"Mom, I gotta tell you."

"What?"

"Everyone's all weird about next year."

"What do you mean?"

"Well, they're out of money, plus they're in debt for this last year. So as they sign up for next year, they don't have any money for that, either. Everybody's depressed."

"What about you?"

"I've made it! It's close, but I'll end this year with about $200 in the black. I'm excited about next year."

"Praise God!"

"Yeah, and my friends are all asking me how I did it."

"Now, these are the friends who felt sorry for you earlier, right?"

"Exactly. So I told them they need to plant their money in a God pot and watch it grow!"

" 'Bring the whole tithe into the storehouse . . . . Test me in this,'
says the Lord Almighty, 'and see if I will not throw open the flood-
gates of heaven and pour out so much blessing that you will not
have room enough for it.' " —Malachi 3:10

With this confidence Cason pressed on, though he would spend the next three years dangling over the flames of financial hell like a marshmallow over a campfire.

If you look back to his money sources for the first year, you'll realize that "savings," "scholarship," and "graduation gifts" were one-time-only amounts. How could he make it through three or four more years? Grandparents contributed, but it still didn't add up.

> *"Wait for the Lord; be strong and take heart and wait for the Lord." —Psalm 27:14*

Toward the end of years two and three, Cason didn't have quite enough to make the last couple of payments. We did two things: 1) We advanced him our parent contribution money. (Normally, we didn't have any extra in the checking account. But when this time came, God had somehow provided extra, so we could offer an advance.) And 2) We offered him a small promise-to-pay. I distinguish these promises-to-pay from loans. These are small amounts, interest free, for a very short time, given to responsible family members. It seemed wasteful to drop out in the middle of the quarter and lose credits. Also, if Cason were no longer a student, he would not be allowed to remain in our health insurance program. The complication and cost of changing health insurance seemed unreasonable, if he were, in fact, able to return to school in the fall.

While we didn't think it was our obligation to fund the kids' college costs (or even bail them out of a jam), we did see ourselves as a team. We had cooperated together during our earlier financial devastation. We had all bitten the bullet. So we were willing to juggle our assets to help them whenever we could.

Cason began a summer job at church camp and immediately handed over most of every paycheck to us, to eliminate the debt.

This is key.

The temptation would have been to stay in debt to Mom and Dad. After all, if you spend your summer salary paying them back, you have zero to start the school year, right?

Right.

And that's what happened. He had almost nothing when school started. Most of the parent contribution we'd advanced for the summer and most of his summer salary had come back to us as a repay. He returned to OU anyway.

I know it sounds ridiculous. But I promised to tell you exactly what we did.

It gets worse.

After one Christmas he returned to school with only $150, knowing that in three weeks he'd have a $900 school payment due. Cason made his payment, and I'm sure The God Factor was involved; but, honestly, none of us remembers exactly where the money came from. We do recall a number of ways financial rescue occurred at various times: There were belated Christmas gifts; shares of Dad's year-end bonus; there were some times when a tax refund came to the rescue; or money was found in a coat pocket; and even—you thought it only happened in a Monopoly game— "bank error in your favor!" I once received an inheritance from an aunt, which I shared with the children, as well. All Cason clearly remembers is that, when he was writing that $900 check, he was thinking, "This can't be possible."

Cason's friends were amazed to learn he was back on campus with only $150. "We wouldn't even have enrolled," they said, "if we didn't have enough to at least finish the quarter."

But we had decided this: It's OK to drop out; but we won't drop out till the last possible moment. We will not act on panic, but will give the Lord a chance to provide.

That last moment came close many times.

"Do not be afraid. Stand firm . . . . The Lord will fight for you;
you need only to be still." —Exodus 14:13, 14

Cason continued to work part-time. After the work-study job, he worked at the athletic center, in the school's telecommunications office, refereed basketball, assisted his DJ friend and finally worked at a local restaurant. These were all no-car-needed jobs.

We encouraged him not to work to the extent that his grades suffered. He was making good grades. It seemed to us that many students were defeating their whole purpose of being in school by working so much they couldn't complete homework assignments.

"In vain you rise early and stay up late, toiling for food to eat—
for he grants sleep to those he loves." —Psalm 127:2

Cason's clothing situation was always alarming, though you probably wouldn't have noticed. A popular "people person," Cason could get away with wearing the same outfits over and over. On the last day of sophomore year, though, his meager wardrobe had deteriorated to almost nothing. While the few items he had gave the appearance that he was dressed presentably, if you held the cloth up to the light, the effect was rather like looking through a screen door. He was scheduled to report for work at camp the next day. So, on the way home, we stopped at a store to replenish his supply. I had not been aware of the strain he'd been under, trying to make his clothing last till the end of the school year. As we left the store, the relief and gratitude poured out: "Oh, this is wonderful!" "I'm so happy!" "You have no idea...."

Cason never had much financial breathing room. And yet, amazingly, he took trips to Chicago, Pittsburgh, Canada, and Florida with his buddies; found a way to backpack through Europe after his third year; and played an occasional paintball game.

We do not understand how the money stretched. We only understand Matthew 6:33. God means what he says. It's just as Cason stated, "We shouldn't have to prove this plan works—but we *have* proved it."

Last week we sat in the auditorium at OU and watched Cason graduate.

One of the speakers addressed the graduates, "...and now it's time to get out in the real world and start paying back those student loans."

"Not me!" Cason shouted back.

Even before graduation, Cason was offered a manager's job at the restaurant near campus, where he had been working. He's decided to take that for now, as a good opportunity in between graduation and going for a "real" career. After this...? He has a comfortable apartment just across the street there where he houses his *Star Wars* collection. By the way, Cason still doesn't own a car—he says he's going for the record. Sometimes he rents one. And he chips in for gas when he shares a ride with friends.

Cason is free.

IN CASON'S OWN WORDS: **Relax and take a deep breath. Just when you think you've hit bottom, realize that it isn't that bad. I tell myself this every day and you'd think I would have learned by now; it is hard. But I have grown to like my "live from paycheck to paycheck" lifestyle. If any new opportunity were to suddenly come up, there really aren't that many things holding me back from making big decisions on the fly. I like the flexibility—not being tied down to twelve credit cards, school/car/house loans, and other debt-related restrictions.**

If you must have a credit card, only have one. Always pay dues on time. Drink plenty of water. Always give your God Money. And stay out of debt at all cost, even if it means moving somewhere else.

"Trust in the Lord with all your heart and lean not on your own understanding; in all your ways acknowledge him, and he will make your paths straight." —Proverbs 3:5, 6

Chapter 4 — Clinton's Story

"Earning Interest!"

Clinton has always had a knack for accumulating money, which his more frivolous friends probably find annoying.

He can recall purchasing a little stuffed pig at the department store when he was five. He remembers how proud he was of himself for being able to pay for the toy out of money he'd saved.

Things haven't changed much.

By his sophomore year in high school Clinton had a sizeable savings account—built only from birthday and Christmas gift money and his very small allowance. His weekly allowance in seventh grade was $1.45; and annual "cost-of-living" increases were meager. But he was generous when it came to buying gifts. He was also careful with his money—and it multiplied.

"His master replied, 'Well done, good and faithful servant!
You have been faithful with a few things; I will put you in
charge of many things.'" —Matthew 25:21

He had watched Karis complete several years of college without loans and felt he'd do OK, too. However, as Cason prepared for college and seemed to be scrambling for money, Clinton became anxious and wondered if he should crank up some more funds. That one summer following his high school sophomore year, he worked full-time at the movie theater.

After that, though, he calmed down and didn't have other summer jobs. He felt he deserved the time off. You see, during school Clinton worked very hard on grades. He also devoted hours of practice time to improving his trombone and piano skills. He knew that doing well in these areas would benefit him in college. Being on the high school tennis team provided a diversion from the academic pressures.

The summers involved two weeks of band rehearsal/camp and a week of tennis camp. Additionally, after his junior and senior years, he spent two weeks in Solid Rock, a music tour group sponsored by Cincinnati Bible College.

Because he worked so hard during the school year and had several summer responsibilities, he spent the rest of the summer just goofing off. Must be nice? He'll say it was.

Jesus said, "Come with me by yourselves to a quiet place and get some rest." —Mark 6:31

The reward was numerous academic scholarships, some renewable for several years. And he received music scholarships from Cincinnati Bible College for his piano and trombone performances in competition.

With all that and the promise of Mom and Dad's allowance, Clinton was financially set way ahead of time for his first year of college.

He packed up his little stuffed pig—yes, the same one—and his *new* "toy," a $1200 trombone—yes, he bought it himself—and headed for college.

Mom and Dad breathed a sigh of relief, but, amazingly, Clinton didn't.

He had all he needed, he'd watched his sister and brother manage on less…so what was the problem?

This is how Satan works. Even though Clinton could see that he was fine for the first year, Satan was right there breathing down his neck, "Yeah, well, what about after that?" And Clinton, being a math whiz, a planner and a worrier, took the bait. He began to calculate ahead to his sophomore and junior years. He could easily conclude that there wouldn't be enough over the long haul.

Satan "is a liar and the father of lies." —John 8:44

It was crisis-of-faith time. Clinton could not ride on Karis and Cason's coattails of faith or even on Mom and Dad's assurance that things would work out. Clinton had to develop his own reliance on God. Even with that fat bank account, Clinton needed to learn that God is the provider, no matter what the account balance says.

Clinton could have gone to either of two bad extremes:

1) continual worry that the money would run out, or
2) overconfidence in the money he had, either
   a) recklessly spending it, or

b) selfishly hoarding it

Thankfully, Clinton made a very wise decision about his money. He continued to be careful. This guy travels light and doesn't do much impulse buying! But he also gave away large amounts of God Money to mission projects and friends in need. He has helped several student friends buy new musical instruments.

"A generous man will prosper; he who refreshes others will himself be refreshed." —Proverbs 11:25

That's a key point.

By giving generously to meet immediate needs, a person is not only acting out Matthew 6:33 but also the next advice from the Creator:

"Do not worry about tomorrow." —Matthew 6:34

This is being (to borrow a phrase from Oswald Chambers) "carefully careless."

The first three years of college, Clinton was in a singing group that traveled on behalf of the school—many weekends and most of the summers. Being in this group meant receiving a tuition grant. That grant, added to the renewable scholarships, has taken care of most expenses. Our allowance money to him is usually left to sit in the bank. The money he earned giving piano lessons one evening a week last year also went into the bank.

Clinton doesn't need to spend much for clothes—free outfits are included in the singing group package; and he likes to shop at thrift stores.

He doesn't need to take vacation trips—the singing group is always traveling, trips which combine work and a little play.

Clinton doesn't even need to buy the occasional magazine to read. Apparently, he has the knack of accumulating magazine subscriptions, as well as money. Really. He is receiving subscriptions to a car magazine, a computer magazine, and a science magazine. He enjoys reading and sharing them—but has no idea where they're coming from!

At times, Clinton has had the means to pay cash for a good used car. He has always *loved* cars. But, even though it wasn't easy, he put that desire on hold since he doesn't actually *need* one. Failure to put desires on hold has caused some of Clinton's classmates to get in over their heads. Some students take out loans that total more than their school bills. These amounts go into the students' accounts. Seeing what looks like a balance, these students feel that they have extra money in their accounts.

Such students go to the business office and ask for that extra money in cash. The temptation is to use it to buy fun stuff—and that's what they do. They use this money as mad money. They buy video games. Or they use the money toward a nicer car, probably not a need. Sometimes the money is spent on eating out or activities that cost—even though they've already paid for the school cafeteria meals and there are numerous free activities available.

"I have learned to be content whatever the circumstances."
—Philippians 4:11

As far as Clinton's schedule, maintaining high grades is a must to keep the renewable scholarships coming. As a music degree candidate, he is involved in his own recital preparation and other musical productions; he accompanies other music students at their lessons and recitals, which provides a tiny cash honorarium; and the singing group membership carries year-round responsibilities. Clinton has volunteered as a student ambassador, giving campus tours to prospective students. There is not much free time, but that's OK. He loves it.

When Clinton *does* have a day off or two weeks off, he rests and plays. He and friends hang out downtown, go to the $1.50 movie theater, or play board games in the school lounge. The last time he had a week off, he bought a season pass to the Paramount King's Island amusement park and went…EVERY DAY to ride the roller coasters.

"Aren't you going to work during break, Clinton?"

"No."

"What *are* you doing?"

"Earning interest!"

He still has the pig and the trombone. And his newest "toy" is a computer he bought himself. He has fun with it, but uses it for homework, too, and to do music composition work which he could not do in the school's computer lab.

In order to get the most out of his classes without overloading, Clinton's undergrad work will require a fifth year. The scholarships will be gone by then; he'll probably need a car, especially if he opts to do a church music internship; he wants to join a church history tour of Europe (he loves architecture) but it costs $3000; he's even considering graduate school.

Where in the world will the money come from?

Clinton isn't worried. *He* doesn't know; but he knows God knows.

Clinton is free.

And, hey—he could always sell some of the assets God has given him: the computer, the trombone, the pig…. Uh-uh, *not* the pig. Don't even go there.

IN CLINTON'S OWN WORDS: **OK, I admit it: I saved money even when I was little. It wasn't that I had any big purchases in mind; I just liked watching the jar fill up. I was fascinated by how saving small amounts of money added up.**

After I participated in the high school All Ohio State Honors Band, I had the opportunity to attend an inexpensive state school, with the probability of a full scholarship. In that scenario, I could have used my savings to buy a car, some nice clothes and accumulate a lot of cool stuff for myself.

But spiritual times in Solid Rock helped me question my attitude. I realized that choosing a college based on how much money I could spend for cool stuff wasn't very wise.

You might think I've had it easy—that having money equals being worry free. But I have found it to be a problem. It's a temptation to throw caution to the wind and just spend it all! I believe God has allowed me to have money so that I will use it for good. Pressure! That's why I make a point of giving it away. I don't want to love it or depend on it. And I don't want to have the attitude, "Hey, I've done enough; I deserve to live rich."

Money can control you—whether you have any or not—

because if you think money is the answer to all your problems, then money is your god. The true God, the creator and sustainer of the universe, doesn't deserve to be pushed aside by money. So look to him when you make decisions.

Chapter 5 — Arian's Story

"I'll live on rice and water if you'll just let me go."

The kids' cousin Arian comes next.

She did some babysitting, and worked as a camp counselor the summer after junior year. She had a savings account of about $1000. But mostly what Arian had done was maintain good grades in high school. And she had developed an impressive resume in set design by working in school plays, church productions and community theater.

So it's not surprising that her portfolio, which reflected her experience and hard work, appealed to the University of Cincinnati's College Conservatory of Music admissions panel. They wanted her talent and noted that few freshmen have had so much experience. UC is one of the top schools in the nation for this program. Competition is tough. Unfortunately, Arian received no talent-based scholarships.

Arian did place high in UC's Cincinnatus (academic scholarship) contest, earning a $5000-a-year award. She also garnered a few small scholarships (local and church) and a couple of small grants.

Even though more was needed, she opted not to do the fast food thing for summer work after her senior year. Instead she felt it more important to work in her field, despite the fact that the work wasn't full-time and the pay was relatively low.

> *"I will praise the Lord, who counsels me . . . .*
> *I will not be shaken." —Psalm 16:7, 8*

Arian lived across the Ohio River in northern Kentucky. So she was looking at a $17,000+ out-of-state price tag for freshman year. The family had recently been through a divorce. Arian's dad gave her a sizeable chunk of money from the sale of the family home. But it didn't seem likely that her single mom would have much cash available. Arian's mom *was* able to contribute by moving to Cincinnati so Arian could switch to the in-state charges of about $10,000. But that would not go into effect until the middle of the next year.

Arian, like her cousins, had the money she needed when the bills were due. She enrolled and began classes at UC.

Toward the end of freshman year, her financial situation was pretty dreary. To make matters worse, Arian had deliberately made summer plans that would bring in zero income!

Here's how it happened:

When Arian was a toddler, her parents had taken her along on a singing tour in Japan. Since age four, she delighted in looking at those photo albums and dreamed of going back to Japan someday.

When she heard of Campus Crusade for Christ's summer projects with international students, she thought that would be a good first step. But Arian had misunderstood the set-up. When she applied for the project she assumed it'd be like other CCC projects where you work a summer job in the day and do ministry with your team during free time. After being accepted, she discovered that international projects had a different format: The entire summer was devoted to the project, with no chance to earn money.

To further complicate matters, the Columbus Ohio international project was cancelled, leaving only the Seattle project. Farther away. More expensive.

Arian grieved over "what I want" vs. "what I should do" vs. "what about money." But, in the middle of all the angst, she kept seeing and hearing things about Seattle: in the news, from her cousin Karis who had moved there, in class...even on T-shirts and bumper stickers. She felt she was being pulled toward the Seattle project.

Finally, she relaxed, deciding that if God wanted her to go, he'd provide the money.

"Commit to the Lord whatever you do, and your plans will succeed." —Proverbs 16:3

The entire $3000 was raised, mostly through donations from family and church friends. Arian knew she wouldn't have enough money to return to school, but she didn't care if she'd have to drop out and work for a while. She was doing the right thing now.

Arian made many Japanese friends in Seattle and loved teaching them about God. At the end of this summer, the entire family planned a fun bonus: Arian's mom and sister and my family flew to Seattle. We visited Karis; then rented a van, picked up Arian and drove back to Ohio through purple mountain majesties and amber waves of grain. Great trip.

Arian had about three weeks till classes started. She had moved into an apartment, having figured that to be more economical than living in the dorm. She had a little cash, a few paying art and theatrical assignments. Still, this doesn't sound like enough.

And it wasn't.

Financial chaos consumed the first quarter of Arian's sophomore year. She couldn't seem to make any money. When she earned a little money, she lost it all on parking tickets and expired tags. When she tried to sell plasma, the donor centers were either shut down or not accepting donations. Her church hired her to do some youth work for which they would pay her $500—but not until December. Arian reached the lowest point when her checkbook showed a "balance" of minus $4.

(Be aware that, when you do something wild for God, Satan is right there to throw marbles under your feet. It's as if that little voice is saying, "See how stupid you were. Serving God was a big mistake. Things can't work out now. You're going down!" But hold on—The God Factor is still in effect.)

Beyond the financial difficulties, this quarter had been an emotional one. Arian missed her Japanese friends terribly and had such a desire to see them over Christmas break, she would have done anything short of selling a kidney to get back to Seattle. Spending Christmas break in Seattle would give her another chance to mentor her Japanese "disciples" in person before they returned to Japan. She was praying and not spending any money. She had gone into a sort of fasting mode and bargained with God: "I'll live on rice and water if you'll just let me go." Arian prayed constantly about this; and, even though the financial situation was bleak and getting bleaker, she had a strange confidence that she would be able to see her friends again.

"Faith is being sure of what we hope for." —Hebrews 11:1

Karis in Seattle had come to know these same Japanese friends and heard one of them mention Arian's wish to see them. In mid-December, Karis contacted Arian: "I think God wants you to come to Seattle during Christmas break. I'll buy your ticket, up to $400 or so."

What followed this offer was a 48-hour frenzy of ticket shopping. Arian's dad had found a bargain ticket earlier, but it was now too late. The cheapest ticket available seemed to be $1200. Then Arian's dad suddenly remembered that he had a stand-by ticket to Louisville someone had given him for $150. He was able to have it switched to Seattle. Arian was on the plane a few days later—and made *all* her stand-by connections. She eventually paid for this ticket herself.

"He fulfills the desires of those who fear him." —Psalm 145:19

After Christmas, Arian's in-state rate kicked in. It turned out that her school bills were completely covered with scholarships.

Plus, for the next two quarters, she would receive cash back in the amount of $1100 from overpay. (Arian had assumed that, if she should be fortunate enough to have the bills covered, any overpay would simply be lost.) Additionally, she was asked to be in charge of set design for one of the main stages, a paid project usually assigned to upperclassmen.

In the rare instances when Arian is actually earning money, she tithes it. She also devotes many hours of her time volunteering in youth ministry work at her church.

Clothing is often taken care of, because Arian has a roommate who buys cool clothes and tires of them quickly.

For fun, Arian and friends enjoy creative and cheap activities: practical jokes on each other that send everyone all over Greater Cincinnati looking for clues; all-night swimming parties and bonfires; camping, theme parties, movie nights and hour-long pillow fights. Plus, in connection with the youth work at her church, she goes on their outings (hayrides, concerts, etc.) as a sponsor.

She finished up her sophomore year just fine.

But—here we go again—she wanted to spend this summer in Japan with Campus Crusade's Kyoto student project. And, to add to the expense, she determined to make a side trip to Tokyo and visit her Japanese student friends from last year in Seattle. We're talking a price tag of $5000 and again, no money earned during the summer for school.

Arian presented her plan to her church. Donations covered the entire amount for her summer expenses.

There are now about "12 disciples" in Arian's group of Japanese student contacts. She takes this ministry seriously and stays in touch with them, trying to lead them closer to God.

(Update: Because of my magic ability to fast forward, I can add some details Arian didn't know going into her junior year. She will work mid-August to mid-September and will earn about $800. The financial aid office is going to call and say Arian's eligible for a grant she somehow missed the paperwork on, bringing her total UC overpay amount up to $1355 per quarter. She will have occasional paying jobs during the year. And here's a fun one: Way back in high school Arian had won a contest for designing a ring. She was to have received a $400 prize, but didn't. That money will arrive soon—three years overdue, but just in time.)

At this point, Arian is on track with her four-year degree program, though it wouldn't matter to her if it took longer to graduate.

Either way, Arian is free.

IN ARIAN'S OWN WORDS: **I would never trade the excitement of living by faith on the "financial edge" and seeing God come through time after time for the false assurance that loans give you. The past two years have been a roller coaster of financial highs and lows, but my life has been better than I ever thought it could be. God used that quarter when I was eating rice every day and struggling to pay my bills to humble me and glorify himself. In turn, he answered those four months of prayer and rice with an amazing last-second trip to Seattle in December that I'll never forget. Each time a check comes in I know God is showing me he is real in a tangible way.**

Chapter 6 — Andrea's Story

A sort of "just God and me" adventure

Arian's sister Andrea just graduated from high school, so her adventure is only beginning.

Here's her background:

Andrea worked throughout high school, both during the year and in the summers, babysitting (private, country club child care and YMCA child care). She also worked at a car wash. Then she filled in at a coffee shop, which turned into a full-time summer job with the promise of future work during college vacation times.

As you'll see in a minute, though, Andrea's savings don't reflect the amount of money she earned. She spent a lot. In my opinion she was somewhat shortsighted and impulsive, spending without looking to her future and the bigger goal. Still, in fairness to her, and to make sure you have a clear picture: In the aftershock of the family's divorce Andrea sometimes ended up paying for her own food and clothing and other necessities. These losses were not her fault.

Divorce rates being what they are, a good number of young readers may have been put in this position. With tension high in both homes, it's often easier for the student to use her own money than to try and decide which parent to ask for money. So student savings have been or are being eaten away due to circumstances beyond the student's control. Parents, in the middle of their own pain, may not even be fully aware of the extent to which their students are paying for their own daily needs.

Parents, it's your job to provide for your children's material needs. Period.

> *"If anyone does not provide for his relatives,*
> *and especially for his immediate family,*
> *he has denied the faith and is worse than an unbeliever."*
> *—1 Timothy 5:8*

It may be time to do a little double-checking.

And, students, try not to grieve over what has been lost. In the end it doesn't matter, because the Lord can compensate for the loss in ways you haven't even dreamed of. Trust him. Do your best. It'll be OK.

> *"Even youths grow tired and weary, and young men stumble and*
> *fall; but those who hope in the Lord will renew their strength. They*
> *will soar on wings like eagles; they will run and not grow weary,*
> *they will walk and not be faint." —Isaiah 40:30, 31*

As for activities, Andrea played a little softball and ran track. But most extra-curriculars focused on using her number one gift: her voice. At age seven she was one of the kid voices on a vacation Bible school song tape for Standard Publishing. She has continued to develop this gift through church choir, drama, singing gigs, as well as in school choir and school plays—her most memorable role starring as Audrey in "Little Shop of Horrors."

Church youth group events took some time, as did Young Life in which she became very active.

Grades? Andrea always had good grades. But the chaos after the divorce seemed to affect her focus. Sometimes her grades plummeted. But she managed to graduate with a 3.2 GPA—enough to wear honors cords for commencement.

Andrea had narrowed her college choices to Baldwin-Wallace (she liked their music/musical theater program) and Cincinnati Bible College (she loved the voice teacher and would be close enough to her old high school area to continue helping Young Life there).

In the end she chose Baldwin-Wallace. She was one of the 10 selected from among 200 applicants for the vocal performance program. She also felt pulled to be away from the familiar, to launch out in a sort of "just God and me" adventure.

"The Lord your God carried you . . . all the way you went until you reached this place." —Deuteronomy 1:31

The actual total yearly cost of Baldwin-Wallace is around $20,000. But the school has offered grants and scholarships to bring that down to $11,000. Andrea has $1200 in local scholarships and $2200 personal money. Her parents have arranged to make up the rest for the first year. (I don't know how Andrea's dad plans to pay his half. Andrea's mom expects to take another job or dip into her savings.)

Andrea's going for a Bachelor of Music degree in vocal performance, with a minor in psychology. She will earn a little money during school; she's been awarded a work-study job (as stage manager, assisting recitals and other music performances). And she's found a very thrifty source for clothes: "shopping" for retro outfits in Granny and Papa's closet!

But can she make it financially?

We can predict neither what events may occur nor what choices Andrea will make. But we know this: Andrea can follow the example of the other four kids. She has everything they had: same information, same Scripture.

And so do you!

"Your word is a lamp to my feet and a light for my path."
—Psalm 119:105

IN ANDREA'S OWN WORDS: **I'm fairly new with all this trust-God-with-your-money thing. Not much experience to speak from. But I think it's Proverbs 3:5, 6 that says: "Trust in the Lord with all your bank account." Or is it "...college tuition?" Pretty soon I won't have any money left. But I'm not too worried. He's proved himself in others areas. So, we'll see....**

Chapter 7 — If You're in Junior High

After reading the student stories, do you think you're on track with the plan from Matthew 6:33:

- putting God first?
- doing what's right?
- trusting God to provide?

Here are things you can start doing now that will help when you reach college—and they hardly hurt at all!

REVIEW. Maybe you haven't been giving the Lord part of your money. Maybe you haven't even been thankful for your money and your stuff. Maybe you have been wasteful with those things. Or selfish.

Don't feel too badly. You're still young. And, unfortunately, some parents don't manage *their* money and stuff very well, either. But if you want to be right with the Lord (and start acting like an adult), then you have to take responsibility for your own money and other belongings.

REVISE. We'll sneak another "R" word in here that will help us REVISE: repent. This means turning yourself around to do better. Ask the Lord to help you see mistakes you made in the past. Tell him you're sorry you messed up. And ask him to lead you in making a new start. This new start calls for some changes in the way you think and act about your money and your stuff.

What if you began thinking of your money and stuff as if it didn't belong to you…as if it really belonged to God? You are just going to manage it for him.

> *"The earth and everything in it belong to the Lord."*
> —*Psalm 24:1, New Century Version*

Surprise! It DOES belong to him. We are just the managers. Our job, then, is to use the money and the stuff as he would want.

MONEY

It may help you to label three jars for your money: God Money, Spend, Save. When you receive any money, go ahead and divide it into the jars. Better yet, have your parents help you open a student savings account at the bank for the "Save" money. You are saving this toward college. Don't bother it except for emergencies.

Examples—

Emergency: your friend's house burns down

Not an emergency: you want a mocha latte

If you don't receive a weekly allowance, ask your parents for one. Explain why you want it. They may ask you to do chores for it. That's all right. (Hey, they're not wrong about *everything.*)

OK, got it?

1 - God Money - I recommend at least 10% of any money you receive

2 - Spend - on gifts for others and some things for yourself

3 - Save - for college

Another point on money: Be totally honest about it.

If you borrow from a friend, pay it back.

If you break something, pay for it.

If you find money, turn it in to Lost & Found.

If the check-out lady gives you too much change, give it back.

This kind of living pleases the Lord—and it makes you feel good.

STUFF

Many junior highers have way too much stuff. (You may have noticed this last year when you tried to clean your room.) Did you ever wonder why you can have everything you need for a week of camp in one suitcase, but at home you have to have 20 times that much in your room? Hmmm.

"Do not store up for yourselves treasures on earth, where moth and rust destroy, and where thieves break in and steal. But store up for yourselves treasures in heaven, where moth and rust do not destroy, and where thieves do not break in and steal. For where your treasure is, there your heart will be also." —Matthew 6:19-21

A responsible manager should handle his stuff, as well as his money, wisely.

Ask your parents if you can REVISE your room and get rid of some stuff. We used the dump method:

1. Dump everything you own into the middle of your floor. Brace yourself. It's awful.
2. Examine your storage space. And get rid of some of it. Most people fill up whatever shelves, drawers and boxes they have. So if you eliminate some of the spaces, it will force you into keeping less stuff.
3. Now you have your storage space ready for what you need. Start putting back only the things you need or want badly.
4. Make two stacks for the other stuff: "trash" and "still good."
5. Throw away the trash.
6. Give away or sell the good used stuff.
7. Put any money you make in your three jars.

Doesn't that feel great?

Now that you've seen how much stuff you accumulated—that you didn't need—be careful when you go shopping. Don't add to what you have. Only buy to replace things that are worn out. If you have 15 T-shirts, only buy a new one if you're willing to throw one out, so you stay at 15.

At this point, I'd like us to take a little sidetrack.

Even though you're just in junior high, you've studied enough math to know that selling your stamp collection and a couple of old sweaters isn't going to add up to the thousands of dollars you need for college. So, why bother with all this little stuff?

I mentioned the story of the feeding of the 5,000 (John 6:1-13) back on page 18 of this book. The child in the story may have been younger than you, but he's the hero. Let's look at it. If you can grasp the key point of this story—and I believe you can—you will be way ahead of your friends (and many adults, too).

The scene: Five thousand people, time to eat, and not a golden arch in sight. One child offered his lunch to Jesus. Why bother? Did he actually think it could help the entire crowd? Or maybe he wanted Jesus to eat it himself. Whatever. The child somehow knew it was the right thing to turn over what little he had to Jesus.

The adults thought the boy's action was silly. "What good is this gonna do?" they said. But they were wrong, weren't they? The Lord took the one lunch and multiplied it into the world's largest picnic!

Don't think of clearing out your stuff as "getting rid of it." Think of it as "handing it over to the Lord."

Now, that doesn't mean you'll put your old bicycle in the offering plate at church Sunday! But ask the Lord to help you decide what to do with your stuff, so that it will go to the "right" place— whether you're selling it or giving it away. Then your part of that is done. What happens next is up to him.

Some people will think you're being silly. "What good is this gonna do?" they'll ask. But they're wrong. They're forgetting about The God Factor.

RELAX. If you haven't been very responsible with your money and your stuff, it may be hard at first to get on track. Give yourself a boost by reading the entire Matthew 6:33 passage, starting with verse 25. The Lord doesn't want us worried. He loves us and wants to give us what we need. (But he cheats—he always gives us more!) If you put him first and do what's right about your money and your stuff, then you can RELAX.

> *"Relax, because the Lord takes care of you."*
> —*Psalm 116:7, New Century Version*

He'll give you what you need PLUS some happy surprises you never even thought of. I know. It happened to us.

Chapter 8 — If You're in High School

Read through the junior high section to REVIEW your own attitudes about money and possessions. Repent of wrong habits and REVISE them—so you can RELAX and trust the Lord.

Here are a few tips just for high schoolers:

MONEY

Have you been living like a millionaire, wildly tossing money around? Guess what? That's not how millionaires live. Thomas J. Stanley studied how the wealthy live. He found that the most successful weren't "spending" money; they were "investing" it. For example, many did not live in the posh neighborhoods or drive the luxury cars you'd expect. They opted not to "spend" on something just for flash; but rather to "invest" in things that earn interest or would, in some other way, be worth more later.[11]

The little things add up. If you will drink water with your school lunches instead of buying a drink, that can total $700 over four years. (Karis's friends laughed at her for drinking water. But when they went into debt for college they weren't laughing.) It's tough bucking the crowd. But you should know that "following the crowd" is one of the "Seven Money Mistakes Everyone Makes."[12] The crowd is often wrong.

"Of what use is money in the hand of a fool, since he has no desire to get wisdom?" —Proverbs 17:16

You see, Karis's friends "bought" drinks. But Karis didn't think drinks were a good "investment;" they didn't have a long-term value. If you can readjust your thinking and substitute the word "invest" for "buy" and "spend," you'll be smarter about the ways you use your money.

Now, as for earning money:

Should you work during the school year? Careful here.

If you spend time on homework to make top grades, you ARE working. Those grades = scholarships = money.

If you use your talents in the school band or on the school softball team, you ARE working. (You aren't employed, but you're working—that is, not being lazy.)

Your main job is to be a good student. It's not your job to earn a living. And you don't have to be involved in every single extracurricular activity. If you spread yourself too thin, you may end up not doing your best at anything. This violates one of God's guidelines:

"Whatever you do, work at it with all your heart, as working for the Lord." —Colossians 3:23

Now, if you can manage a side job, go ahead. For Karis, studies came rather easily; so she didn't jeopardize her grades while earning a little money at the library job. You should pursue things you excel in. And do some things that stretch you. But don't overwork...OR overplay.

STUFF

Have you ever walked the mall without buying a single thing? Try it. As you window shop, tell yourself:

"The Lord is my shepherd. I have everything I need."
—Psalm 23:1, New Century Version

It's a feeling of power.

Do the clear-out that was suggested in the junior high chapter. (Girls, if three or four of your friends will agree to clear out their closets, you can get together afterwards and have a swap party to trade unwanted clothes. Then throw out some more!)

"I have seen a grievous evil under the sun: wealth hoarded to the harm of its owner." *—Ecclesiastes 5:13*

Then, from here on, focus one eye on college. That doesn't mean you can't do fun things and buy some stuff now. But, with one eye on college, you can evaluate your spending better: "When I'm in college, will I be glad I bought/invested in this?"

High schoolers have some big expenses, like prom clothes, for example. There is nothing wrong with these things. But sometimes we accumulate more of these items than we really need. Cooperate with your parents to help the whole family save.

- Buy used prom clothes or swap last year's with friends.
- Buy four senior picture proofs instead of 12.
- School rings, jackets, yearbooks, graduation paraphernalia: Take a step back emotionally to make wise choices. Which things will still be treasured 10 years from now?
- Of course you want a car. Who doesn't? But do you really need one? Hitch rides with your friends. Pay them for it. They'll be happy and you'll save tons. Choose a summer job you can walk or bicycle to. Share one car between siblings.

"Those who plan and work hard earn a profit."
—Proverbs 21:5, New Century Version

I know high schoolers are super busy. If you feel too busy to take the time to REVIEW and REVISE your habits, it only proves that you need to. Take control. The RELAX part is worth it.

BONUS SECTION FOR HIGH SCHOOLERS

Consider the big picture—the really big picture—when you search for the right college. What would the Lord want for your future? What are your talents, strengths, likes and dislikes? What schools seem to match them?

Don't rule out a school because of the cost. More expensive schools may have more attractive financial aid packages. (Remember Andrea's story.) Think best case scenario, and start taking steps in that direction. Don't be afraid.

Look for creative ways of avoiding debt. Ask about night classes; sometimes they're cheaper. If you're close to home, ask about commuting instead of living in the dorm. If the school you like is far away, ask whether you can live in the dorm, even if you're working and only taking classes part-time. Check out the colleges your parents attended; some give alumni kid scholarships. Earn some credits at a community college, then transfer to complete your degree at the college of your choice. Ask graduating college seniors how they've managed.

Be honest in your search for financial aid. It's very tempting to exaggerate your needs and to minimize how much money you actually have. Don't expect the Lord to help if you're being dishonest. Accurately fill out *all* forms.

"Whoever can be trusted with very little can also be trusted with much, and whoever is dishonest with very little will also be dishonest with much." —Luke 16:10

Even if you're a high school freshman, it's not too early to start a "financial aid possibilities" file. Stick everything related to jobs, scholarships, grants, etc., in there. When you're a junior or senior, it's much easier to start with this file than to be starting from scratch.

Warning: Be on guard when you talk to college representatives at College Day programs. Their job is to make their school appeal to you. They use the term "financial aid" when explaining how much help they can give you. But "financial aid" includes loans as well as scholarships. Many students have been misled, because they didn't understand the lingo. Tell the rep you are not talking loans and simply want scholarship information. He may be in shock for a moment—perhaps no one has ever said this to him before. Then tell him again. Insist on knowing what scholarships or other actual money breaks you may reasonably expect to receive.

There are several places you can start looking for scholarships:

1. Your high school guidance department. They can lead you to various sources.

Our high school published a list of about 25 local scholarships. Some students chose one or two likely sources and applied for those. *My* reasoning went like this: Apply for all of them. Say it takes ten hours to do all the paperwork. Even if you win merely one $1000 scholarship, you invested only ten hours for $1000. That's a $100-per-hour payback. Pretty good money!

By the way, get some help filling out these applications. Parent, guidance counselor, college friend, English teacher . . . . Do it right.

2. Network. Put grandparents on alert to check scholarship possibilities in their newspapers. Team up with your best friend: You keep an eye out for sports scholarships for him, and he watches for physical therapy scholarships for you.

3. The library. The public library has books on scholarships: which schools offer what scholarships, general scholarship possibilities according to field of study, etc. There are also books on how to pay for college. (Trust me, skip the chapters on loans.) Most of these books are located in the area of call numbers 378.3 (Dewey Decimal System). Check it out. And don't be afraid to ask the research librarian for further help. That's her job.

If you go to the trouble of borrowing some of these books, perhaps your parents will help you look through them.

4. Online. Online information tends to change quickly. But, at this writing, a couple of helpful web sites are:

www.fastweb.com — offers a free scholarship search and information on 4,000 colleges

www.finaid.org — explains loans, grants, etc.; offers scholarship search

Or you can run your own search on any search engine using the phrases "financial aid" or "college scholarships."

Beware of companies who offer to do a scholarship search for a fee. These organizations usually promise to locate a certain number of potential "financial aid" sources for you. But financial aid includes loans; so many of the sources will be only loans. Others will be common ones you could easily have learned about through the high school guidance department. The remaining scholarship sources are often pretty unlikely, along the lines of: "One hundred dollar scholarship to children of door-to-door water tower salesmen!"

5. The financial aid department of the college you're interested in They have the power to help you, no matter how the FAFSA report pigeonholed you. Find one helpful person at each school. Then, when you call or write, communicate with that person every time so you develop a rapport. Act like somebody. Don't whine or play pitiful. Statements like:

"I can't afford that."

"There's no way...."

"You gotta be kidding!"

make a poor witness of someone who supposedly trusts the Lord. Say things like:

"Thanks for sending me the green colored scholarship list. Are there other scholarships available?"

"What's your policy on ...?"

"Do you have any ideas about ...?"

"I took your advice and did A, B and C. Is there anything else I should do?"

"I appreciate your help so much."

Apply for every possible scholarship—and a few *impossible* ones. You will not be awarded every scholarship you apply for. In fact, most of the scholarships you apply for will be dead ends. Doesn't mean a thing. Do your best. The Lord of Financial Aid knows what you need. So ask him to take charge of your situation.

Then ...stand back!

Chapter 9 — If You're in College

OK, you're already in college.

And already in debt.

You can sympathize with the student who wrote to me:

> Dear Lynn, Thank you for sharing your insight about financial aid. I wish I would have considered it much sooner. Unfortunately, in my case the damage has already been done.
>
> This is my fifth year of college, and my student loan debt totals $21,000. In addition, I have about $5500 left to pay on my car loan.
>
> I realize I've dug myself into a hole, but I am very willing to do something about it now. I think God has been trying to call my attention to this issue in a variety of ways for some time now. I've been very stubborn!
>
> My tithes have been inconsistent. I always give something, but I know it doesn't represent ten

percent of my income.

I'm going to pray every day for guidance. I know the Lord can still use me in spite of the mistakes I've made in the past and the consequences for those choices. I don't feel hopeless, but very convicted and very challenged to repent and obey. — "B.J."

That letter broke my heart, and I hurt for every one of you in B.J.'s situation. Just imagine how much B.J. will spend on interest over the long haul. (Loan repayments can be calculated online at www.usnews.com/usnews/edu/dollars/dsrepay.htm.)

Now that you understand the principles of this book, you can probably analyze B.J.'s circumstances. What mistakes do you think were made? Here's what I see:

- increased college debt year after year
- added a car loan on top of that
- ignored God's trying to call attention to the problem
- had a too-casual attitude about God Money

So …is it too late for B.J.?
No!

"Surely the arm of the Lord is not too short to save, nor his ear too dull to hear." —Isaiah 59:1

It is NEVER too late to throw yourself on God's mercy.

"I cry aloud to the Lord; I lift up my voice to the Lord for mercy. I pour out my complaint before him; before him I tell my trouble. When my spirit grows faint within me, it is you who know my way. In the path where I walk men have hidden a snare for me. Look to my right and see; no one is concerned for me. I have no refuge; no one cares for my life. I cry to you, O Lord.... Listen to my cry, for I am in desperate need." —Psalm 142:1-6

"Though I have fallen, I will rise. Though I sit in darkness, the Lord will be my light." —Micah 7:8

"The Lord is righteous in all his ways and loving toward all he has made. The Lord is near to all who call on him, to all who call on him in truth . . . . He hears their cry and saves them." —Psalm 145:17-19

The Lord said to Paul, "My grace is sufficient for you, for my power is made perfect in weakness." —2 Corinthians 12:9

"God is our refuge and strength, an ever-present help in trouble. Therefore we will not fear, though the earth give way and the mountains fall into the heart of the sea." —Psalm 46:1, 2

Read the Scriptures again.

And mark this page so you can keep coming back to it. These Scriptures are the evidence that your situation is not impossible. Lean on the Lord's power. Lean hard!

Back to B.J.'s letter. Any points on the plus side? I see that B.J.:

- admits the problem
- is willing to listen to advice
- doesn't blame anybody else
- sees the importance of repenting and obeying
- knows God can work it out

Combine B.J.'s attitude with those Scriptures and…wow! I'm confident B.J. will come out OK on this. Now, what are *you* going to do about your own situation?

Though we did not go into debt for college, we were in equally difficult financial circumstances. I think the solutions are the same.

REVIEW your financial habits so you can REVISE them. Read through the junior high and high school sections of this book, if you haven't already. You'll find help there. You may see areas in which you made big mistakes. Admit them. Even if you feel your parents and counselors were at fault, there came a time when you made the wrong decisions. Tell God you're sorry you didn't:

- manage well
- trust him to provide
- pay your bills on time
- always deal honestly
- thank him ….

My advice is to come to a screeching halt…STOP!…and take steps NOW to put yourself straight financially. And the first step to getting out of debt is to stop going further in.

Have you ever been eating a big slab of gooey cake, when

someone steps up and says, "You know there are 850 calories in every bite of that?!" You have three bites left. What do you do? Most of us finish the cake anyway, determining to do better next time.

I'm suggesting you NOT finish the cake. There's a difference between eating the cake in ignorance, unaware that it's harmful, and continuing to eat it *after* you know. To keep going into debt after you've determined it's harmful can only lead to heartache.

"When a wise person sees danger ahead, he avoids it. But a foolish person keeps going and gets into trouble."
—Proverbs 27:12, New Century Version

Over and over in the Old Testament people lost the opportunity of God's help by continuing to do things they knew he disapproved of. Contrast that attitude with the psalmist's:

"I have considered my ways and have turned my steps to your statutes. I will hasten and not delay to obey your commands."
—Psalm 119:59,60

Hasten. That means hurry.

Dave Ramsey encourages people to be angry enough about their debt to go ahead and do something about it. He tells of "white-collar guys earning $65,000 a year and delivering pizzas at night because they're sick of being in debt."[13] They're hastening.

I know, you can't imagine how everything can work out. It's scary, a bad kind of scary.

Refer back to the commentary for Matthew 6:33, our theme verse, on page 16.

If you're ready to start over, living in accordance with this passage, it's going to involve some God Money.

"But," you might object, "shouldn't I get out of debt first—and then start giving to God once I'm back up to zero? I mean … I'm too bad off to spare anything for God right now."

If that's what you're thinking, then you still don't get it. It's precisely because you're in such trouble that you should start giving some of your money to God immediately. That will indicate an attitude of putting God first, of honoring him, of giving him control, of trusting him and not yourself. Then The God Factor can enter the equation.

And that's a good kind of scary.

Perhaps a real life example will help:

Mary Hunt racked up a debt of over $100,000. But she paid it back. And relatively quickly. When people ask how she managed it, she answers, "We started giving away some of our money," following Scriptural guidelines.

She elaborates: "A funny thing began to happen. More money came in. Greater opportunities presented themselves for me to earn even more, which allowed my husband, Harold, and me to start paying back the debts rapidly. As I look back, I am astounded by the ways God put the pieces of our financial puzzle back together. I couldn't really see it at the time, so it was pure trust that drove me to give."[14]

Pure trust.

You can do the same thing she did. And I imagine, if you start taking steps of trust, the Lord will immediately start helping you make sense of the rest of your puzzle. Maybe you'll feel "nudged" to:

1) not enroll in school next quarter, but work instead
2) sell or give away three-fourths of your stuff
3) correct some little white lies on the paperwork the school has on you
4) tithe retroactively—give the Lord half of last month's income
5) sell the car

But in the next split second, the little demon on your shoulder will be right there whispering rebuttals to each of those thoughts:

1) "maybe enroll for just one more quarter first"
2) "there's no need to go *that* far"
3) "no big deal, everybody does that"
4) "there'll be nothing left!"
5) "yeah, right"

Just because you decide to obey God doesn't necessarily mean all the problems will instantly disappear. Sometimes bad choices have lingering consequences.

You may have to work two years to get out of debt...then go back and finish school. (Although the Lord *could* send you a surprise check today to pay everything off. It depends on his plan and what other lessons he wants you to learn.)

Your dilemma here is whether to stay under the thumb of your creditors or whether to put yourself in the palm of God's hand.

I love the story about David in 2 Samuel 24. David has "done a very foolish thing" (v. 10). The Lord is going to punish him, but lets David choose the punishment. David chooses natural disasters over being chased by his enemies. He says,

"I am in deep distress. Let us fall into the hands of the Lord, for his mercy is great; but do not let me fall into the hands of men."
—2 Samuel 24:14

David got that right. If something unpleasant had to happen, he wanted it to be under God's direction, not man's.

I am comparing this to your current situation. If, like David, you have "done a very foolish thing," the results will almost certainly include some unpleasantness. If you have to pay off student loans till you're 40, that will be unpleasant. But if you put school on hold to get out of debt now, that will be unpleasant, too.

Place yourself in God's hands and don't resent his discipline.

"Don't stop trying when the Lord corrects you. The Lord corrects those he loves." —Hebrews 12:5,6 New Century Version

If you can, look at this as a new adventure, an adventure to which you already know the ending:You win!

"He knows the way that I take; when he has tested me,
I will come forth as gold." —Job 23:10

All the Bible greats—Daniel, Esther, Joseph and your favorite hero—walked some difficult roads. But what adventures they had! You can bet they did not look back on their lives with regret. Sometimes, though, they *did* have to walk alone. You'll recall those Bible stories are not titled:

Daniel and Ricky in the Lion's Den

Brave Esther and Tiffany Challenge the King

Joseph and Buzz Impress the Pharaoh

No, our heroes were on their own. So, if you feel alone and don't receive much human support as you take the higher road, recall their stories as encouragement.

And RELAX. The person who holds God's hand wins.

Always.

Chapter 10 — For Parents Only

Writing this chapter made me nervous.

It's one thing for me to give money advice to young people. It's another for me to give advice from parent to parent. Most of us receive money advice with at least some degree of defensiveness. Frankly, we don't like someone else implying that we haven't been doing our best.

So I want to assure you I don't think any such thing. I assume you *have* been doing your best. But, rare indeed is the person today who can manage to avoid being caught up in our spending society. Many of us parents, who should have been saving for our children's college education (and teaching the children how to save some of their own money, as well) have, instead, been living beyond our means (and teaching our children to do the same). It's the norm these days.

Suddenly, college is upon us, and the coffers are empty.

In the panic we sign up for loans. In other words, there isn't any money for college, but we want our kids to start school this fall with everybody else. We hurtle forward into debt. Or worse, we sign up our children for loans. There is nothing wrong with the student paying his own way for college. The problem comes if we have been poor managers and maxed out our own credit. Then, in a final desperate moment, we allow our children to bail us out of our own failure to manage well.

This can't be right.

"After all, children should not have to save up for their parents, but parents for their children." —2 Corinthians 12:14

Perhaps you've been re-evaluating your own money philosophy and spending habits as you read this book. That's a good start toward helping your children REVIEW, REVISE and RELAX about their own financial circumstances.

As you do your own financial REVIEW, I suggest skimming through this book again, reading only the Scripture passages. They're pretty convicting. Even though money is one of my pet subjects, I still find myself sometimes being snagged by one of these Scriptures with a sudden "Whoa!" It's not fun to discover that you've made financial decisions that were somewhat less than Scriptural.

"You are in error because you do not know the Scriptures or the power of God." —Matthew 22:29

But it's OK. If you see the problems and want to REVISE, the Lord's power is right at your fingertips. An awareness of The God Factor is more important than what the calculator says.

As parents, it's our financial responsibility to:

- trust the Lord, not our employer, as our provider
- be thankful for what he provides
- live within our means
- supply our children's "food and clothing" (their basic needs)
- be good managers for the children to imitate
- be generous with and honest about money, so the children see that lifestyle in action

As you begin to REVISE the areas you're dissatisfied with, don't forget to clear the air with good old-fashioned repentance. Admit to the Lord that you have failed to follow his guidelines. Ask for his forgiveness and for his help and leading as you attempt to straighten things out. Repentance is basically an acknowledging of wrong, an apology and a statement of intent to act differently in the future.

Apologizing to the Lord is not very difficult, really.

Apologizing to your children will be a little tougher. But that's what I suggest.

Children tend to copy their parents' methods. So, if the children haven't been good money managers, they may simply be imitating you. Or, possibly, you taught them well; but they tend to be reckless anyway—and you've been lax in tightening the leash.

At any rate, a family powwow is in order. Explain some of your past financial practices and apologize for the ones you now see as flawed. Discuss how you plan to REVISE your own habits and how you're going to help the children REVISE theirs.

Dave Ramsey says that becoming financially stable is 80 percent behavior modification and only 20 percent knowledge.[15] There will have to be change, if you're serious.

For your younger children, you may have to implement new rules. Help them understand what you're doing and why it will ultimately make life easier for them.

If you have children who are already in debt, you'll need to partner with them to help them get out. It is my personal conviction that an 18-year-old does not realize the significance of going deeply into debt. But we parents *do* realize what it means. If you encouraged your children to go into debt, I think you must bear some of the responsibility for allowing things to reach this unhappy state.

Remember, the purpose of REVIEWing and REVISEing is for the whole family to be able to RELAX about college finances.

I hope these five Ds will help you get your financial ducks in a row:

1) DESIRE God's way. Recognize him as creator and provider. He knows best.

"His divine power has given us everything we need." —2 Peter 1:3

2) DECIDE to put him first. Focus on him instead of money.

"The love of money is a root of all kinds of evil. Some people, eager for money, have wandered from the faith and pierced themselves with many griefs." —1 Timothy 6:10

3) DETERMINE to be completely honest in all financial

matters, regardless of how tempting it is to do otherwise. (And regardless of what other people seem to be getting away with—that's *their* problem.)

"Wealth that comes from telling lies vanishes like a mist and leads to death." —Proverbs 21:6, New Century Version

4) DISTRIBUTE unnecessary possessions by giving away, selling, trading...or trashing. This process not only unclutters your house, it unclutters your head! Amazing.

"Give, and it will be given to you. A good measure, pressed down, shaken together and running over, will be poured into your lap. For with the measure you use, it will be measured to you." —Luke 6:38

5) DON'T WORRY. You've done your part. The rest is up to the Lord. He knows what to do.

"Do not be anxious about anything, but in everything, by prayer and petition, with thanksgiving, present your requests to God."
—Philippians 4:6

PARENTS' NITTY GRITTY:
How to be Your Own Financial Aid Office

We parents have to be savvy about student loans. Cast a suspicious eye toward those pushing you and your students to apply for loans. Who are they? The colleges themselves, the government, the banks and credit card companies. *They will profit from your debt.*

Maybe we should take the bull by the horns and become our own financial aid offices.

Here is some help:

Focus on what you *do* have, not on what you don't have. Remember the little boy's lunch at the feeding of the 5,000. Remember The God Factor.

Make a chart for each of your children, blocking out four years of college costs into monthly payments. Be realistic about the cost. It's not only tuition, room and board, books, fees; don't forget travel expenses, clothing, miscellaneous. Then start filling in the blocks.

MONEY SOURCES:

Of course, you should check out your savings accounts, CDs, stocks and other investments. But those options are beyond the scope of this book. I'm showing you how we did it with none of those resources except the students' own savings.

Summer job money—If your children will work every summer, you can fill in a few squares for each child, for each year. That feels better already, huh?

Student savings—This may be only enough to fill in one square for the freshman year. That's OK. Fill it in.

Scholarships—Fill in these as you learn of them. And be hopeful. There is always the chance your student will receive future scholarship monies. Karis and Arian did.

Parent contribution—We give ours in the form of a weekly allowance. If you can manage $40 a week, that's about $2000 a year. Fill in the squares.

Student job during college—Even if your child can work only 5-10 hours a week during school, he can still come up with $1000 every year.

Other family—Do grandparents plan on assisting your children in college? Grandparents may not realize how matters have changed since they went to college. In "the good old days" a student could pay as he went by working all summer and some during school. The amount he could earn in proportion to reasonable college costs made this possible. Now, though, college costs have soared completely out of proportion to the amount a student can earn. The difference between then and now is staggering. Grandparents might be willing to join the family team effort if they were made aware of the enormous financial challenges the children are faced with. Offer to help grandparents have a big garage sale for a percentage of the profit. (You're going to have to help them clean out that attic one of these days anyway!)

Every family should be able to fill in at least a few of the squares from these sources.

I understand the tendency to believe these small efforts can't possibly add up to much. But it's funny, isn't it? We believe that one extra cookie we ate every day suddenly became 50 extra pounds! We believe those "few" purchases last month turned into a $700 credit card bill. And that one cancer cell grew into an invasive terror. So we do believe the theory when applied to bad things. God has proved over and over that he can multiply little good things into more. But somehow…we don't believe in The God Factor.

According to Dave Ramsey, church attenders aren't much

different from others when it comes to financial problems. "There should be a difference, but there isn't.... The statistics are very, very similar.... I wish we were doing better as Christians, but the reality is that there is very little difference."[16]

Shame on us.

Here are some other options:

This year's vacation—Skip it. Stay home and spend the week in a "College Money Treasure Hunt." Work together to do massive clear-outs: basement, attic, garage. Oh, the things you'll unearth! The idea will be to turn unwanted "assets" into cash to be divided among the children for their college funds. Then split up the money you would have spent on the vacation trip. Talk together about new strategies for managing money. Brainstorm. You may be surprised at how the children rise to the occasion.

Of course, this IS your vacation week. So plan some fun every day: picnic, family tennis tournament, board game marathon, hiking.... Wouldn't it be funny if you finished up this week feeling more rested than if you'd gone to Disney World?

What about your cars?—At one point our family had five drivers on one car. That's drastic! And, frankly, I don't recommend it. But it's also drastic for college students to crank up a debt they can't pay off until they're 40. Can you make some changes regarding your transportation?

Family budget—If your goal is to make money for college, you can find ways to economize. The students in our high school ate their lunches out at local fast food restaurants. We gave our kids a set amount of money, adequate to pay for the week's lunches. But, the deal was that, if they could shop smart and use coupons, they could keep what was left over as their own, supplementing their small allowances. Forced to make daily choices, they learned tremendous management skills this way. If they were careless, it meant that Friday's lunch was reduced to a 59c bean burrito. Or sometimes they made plans with friends to eat at a special place on Friday—so they chose to eat bean burritos the first four days to save up.

This is just one example. You—and your children!— can think of other ways, if you look deeper, for cutting corners on clothing, entertainment, transportation, the phone bill, electricity.

You know, there is a bonus reward to this teamwork. When our financial strain was great, it was difficult to follow the Bible direction:

"Give thanks in all circumstances." —1 Thessalonians 5:18

But now I *am* thankful. I can see that those troubles helped us work together and grow close as a family. And that spirit has filtered down as the children reach out to help each other in college (Karis gave money to Cason, Cason to Arian …).

Insurance—When was the last time you checked your insurance policies: life, health, car and homeowners? Can these be adjusted? Combined? Could you cash in a small policy?

Retirement—Experts usually advise us not to touch retirement money. But check it out. It may be possible for you to withdraw a portion of your retirement funds without really damaging them over the long haul. (We withdrew a little and bonused the kids once.) Do the math. Read the financial advisors quoted in this book.

Garage sale of the century—Imagine you are moving your

family to another state for one year. What would you take with you? These are your necessities. You can sell everything else. Yes, you can! You know what they say: "That which you cannot give away, you do not possess. It possesses you."[17]

> *"We brought nothing into the world,*
> *and we can take nothing out of it." —1 Timothy 6:7*

House—Now, with three-fourths of your stuff gone and the children starting to leave home, can you sell your home and move down? True happiness and success aren't related to the size of your house. Remember,

> *"Our citizenship is in heaven." —Philippians 3:20*

I find it so interesting that former Beatle Paul McCartney (with an estimated fortune of $500 million) and his wife Linda chose to raise their four children in a two-bedroom cottage. "I'm very happy with very little," Linda told *Vanity Fair*. "Maybe that's why I have so much."[18]

After we had lived through six years of debt free college, I began thinking about our house debt. Maybe I wasn't wholeheartedly practicing what I preached. Though touting the necessity of debt free college, had I drawn a line across which I wouldn't trust God to provide?

It seemed to me that people who had $1 couldn't believe in God's ability to provide $1000. Students who had $1000 feared God couldn't give them $10,000 for college. But we had gone into debt for our house, because $100,000 seemed an impossibly large amount to hope for.

I didn't like the implications.

I was ashamed of my own lack of faith. Perhaps I'd never really thought of this as a faith issue before. We had simply secured a 30-year home mortgage like everyone else. That's how it was done.

But Scriptural evidence was against us. The Bible's stand on borrowing is cautious at best:

"The borrower is servant to the lender." —Proverbs 22:7

"The Lord your God will bless you as he has promised, and you will lend to many nations but will borrow from none."
—Deuteronomy 15:6

"Let no debt remain outstanding, except the continuing debt to love one another." —Romans 13:8

Long-term debt is most definitely discouraged:

"At the end of every seven years you must cancel debts."
—Deuteronomy 15:1

Clearly the Lord wants us to use what we have and look to him to multiply it. The story of the widow's oil in 2 Kings 4 illustrates this, as do these Scriptures:

Agur's prayer: "Don't make me either rich or poor. Just give me enough food for each day. If I have too much, I might reject you. I might say, 'I don't know the Lord.' If I am poor, I might steal. Then I would disgrace the name of my God."
—Proverbs 30:8, 9 New Century Version

"We were under great pressure . . . . But this happened that we might not rely on ourselves but on God." —2 Corinthians 1:8, 9

"Help us, O Lord our God, for we rely on you."
—2 Chronicles 14:11

So we sold the house—and have not regretted it.

Using the profit from that sale was fun. There was a big chunk of God Money that benefited several missions. And we gave the kids a huge bonus, a complete surprise to them: "You're getting your inheritance early. Don't mess it up!"

The timing of this event is especially interesting as it relates to Cason. You'll recall that he lived on the financial edge most of the time; and he didn't particularly like it, either.

"Whoever loves money never has money enough; whoever loves wealth is never satisfied with his income." —Ecclesiastes 5:10

But finally he grew to the point where his heart was settled, and he felt satisfied with what he had. THEN he was given this large amount. An amusing highlight to the story: Cason had lived on the brink of zero for so long, he wasn't used to having a bank balance.

This was a strange new feeling for him—and he had to lie down frequently for several months!

* * *

After undergoing this financial evaluation, use the figures you come up with to fill in the blanks on your children's charts.

> *"He who gathers money little by little makes it grow."*
> —*Proverbs 13:11*

Now that you've discovered some different possibilities for paying college costs, how do you view the following situation: Parents of a girl bound for college "this fall" wrote to Mary Hunt, editor of *The Cheapskate Monthly.* Even though their daughter was applying for scholarships, they were concerned. They said they were without "savings or financial resources." And they feared their earnings were too high to qualify for financial aid.

"How do we pay?" they asked. "Should we take out a home equity loan or go for the PLUS loan? She will work all next summer and hopefully will have some money, but she doesn't want to spend it on school. She wants to save her money for the future."[19]

Perhaps it's not fair for us to assess, when we don't know all the details. But let's give it a shot. Here's what I see:

- The parents have already decided to take a loan.
- They haven't considered any time frame other than the daughter's starting school "this fall."

- It is possible that they make too much money to receive need-based financial aid and, at the same time, have no savings or other financial resources. Since the FAFSA people consider only last year's salary, this family could have experienced absolute financial wipe-out two years ago, but had a good salary last year. Call me suspicious, but I think they would have mentioned their devastation and what deserving folks they are, in light of that. (I know *I* did!) So I conclude that—and the odds are, since it's the most common scenario—they have consistently made a decent salary, but have failed to save.

- No "financial resources?" They talk of a home equity loan, so they own a home. That's a financial resource. And, if the home is furnished, that's a financial resource. I have been very sympathetic toward people with financial problems. I know the crushing feeling of not owning so much as a paper clip. But my experience has been that, when people say they "don't have anything," they are, without exception, not telling the truth. Rather, they're simply unwilling to give up or rearrange some of their paper clips!

And what about the daughter?

- It sounds as if she has no money of her own until

she works next summer. Has she not learned to save a little?

- The daughter, not willing to spend any of her own money for her own college expenses, clearly has an entitlement problem. She thinks she is entitled to a college education paid for by others.

In my opinion, this poor girl does not understand money management (or life either, I'm afraid). I predict catastrophe should her parents hand her a free college ride or encourage her to take out a student loan.

How did Mary Hunt answer this question? She suggested the daughter "sit out for a few years while working two or three jobs to achieve the pay-as-you-go method."[20]

She defends this "harsh" response by mentioning the letters she receives from student debtors: newlyweds with a $70,000 debt, credit card debt, babies and jobs that aren't the dream jobs the students had expected. These are desperate young families who seek Ms. Hunt's advice on ways they can have their loans forgiven. (The term "loan forgiveness" can refer to a program in which the debtor works off the debt, via employment with a specific agency for a set number of years. But I felt the context of this article was referring to forgiveness in terms of debt cancellation.) People who are overwhelmed want to wipe the slate clean. But, as Larry Burkett points out, there is no Scriptural allowance for walking out on our debts.[21] While it is legal to declare bankruptcy, the Bible says

"The wicked borrow and do not repay." —Psalm 37:21

The Lord can fix the situation, no matter how impossible it seems. But wouldn't it be smarter to avoid this pain in the first place?

"Student debt," says Ms. Hunt, "can put a family into horrible financial bondage for decades while creating unbearable stress."[22]

Horrible?

Bondage?

Decades?

Unbearable?

Can these words describe what the Lord wants for his children? Rather,

"God can give you more blessings than you need. Then you will always have plenty of everything. You will have enough to give to every good work." —2 Corinthians 9:8, New Century Version

The country's economists and financial experts say, "Get out of debt and stay out." Are we going to ignore both the human experts as well as the Bible's teachings?

Chapter 11 — And Finally . . . .

At the beginning of this book, I mentioned that even atheists could manage to avoid student loans. And that's true. There are plenty of little tips in this book, which will help anyone, regardless of their spiritual beliefs. But I hope I've made it clear that the foundation of our stories was a belief in God and his word. I italicized and centered the Scripture passages so they would stand out; because, to me, they're the most important part of the formula. Tips are helpful. Scripture works.

I'd like to close with a few more powerful verses.

Some of the most phenomenal miracles of all time are recorded during the lifetime of Joshua. For example:

- the crossing of the Jordan at Joshua's command (similar to Moses' crossing of the Red Sea)

"Now the Jordan is at flood stage all during harvest. Yet as soon as the priests who carried the ark reached the Jordan and their feet touched the water's edge, the water from upstream stopped flowing. It piled up in a heap a great distance away . . . . So the people crossed over." —Joshua 3:15, 16

- the fall of Jericho

"The seven priests carrying the seven trumpets went forward, marching before the ark of the Lord and blowing the trumpets . . . . They marched around the city once and returned to the camp. They did this for six days. On the seventh day, they got up at daybreak and marched around the city . . . except that on that day they circled the city seven times. The seventh time around, when the priests sounded the trumpet blast, Joshua commanded the people, 'Shout! For the Lord has given you the city!' . . . When the people gave a loud shout, the wall collapsed; so every man charged straight in, and they took the city." —Joshua 6:13-16, 20

- the day the sun stood still

"Joshua said to the Lord . . . : 'O sun, stand still over Gibeon, O moon, over the Valley of Aijalon.' So the sun stood still, and the moon stopped, till the nation avenged itself on its enemies . . . . The sun stopped in the middle of the sky and delayed going down about a full day. There has never been a day like it before or since, a day when the Lord listened to a man." —Joshua 10:12-14

Can river water really pile up in a heap? Of course not. Can trumpets and shouting bring down a city wall? I don't think so. Can a man order the sun to stop? Impossible! But

"Nothing is impossible with God." —Luke 1:37

There it is again: The God Factor. These events *did* happen to Joshua—and we know how! The secret to Joshua's success is plainly explained to us in Joshua 1. The Lord, when commissioning Joshua to replace Moses, said:

"Be strong and very courageous. Be careful to obey all the law my servant Moses gave you; do not turn from it to the right or to the left, that you may be successful wherever you go. Do not let this Book of the Law depart from your mouth; meditate on it day and night, so that you may be careful to do everything written in it. Then you will be prosperous and successful. Have I not commanded you? Be strong and courageous. Do not be terrified; do not be discouraged, for the Lord your God will be with you wherever you go." —Joshua 1:7-9

It may not be easy, but debt free college is pretty simple.

- Obey the Lord's commands. Strictly.
- Press on without fear.
- Then The God Factor comes into play, to insure success.

I have a little crush on Joshua. Wasn't he something? But he was just an ordinary person who followed God more closely than the rest of us do. People like Joshua aren't lucky, somehow singled out to have all the breaks, all the adventure. People like Joshua trust God more. That's why miracles happen to them.

The members of my family will tell you that none of us has Joshua's faith. We don't obey God's commands perfectly. And we have sometimes let fear hold us back. (Remember how miserably I failed at "do not be terrified" when we were beginning Karis's college preparations?)

But the Lord's power, his mercy and generosity are just bursting at the seams. I believe he answers even our most feeble attempts to trust him. The priests at the Jordan River trusted the Lord to stop the water. They didn't wait for it to stop and then step in. They stepped in first. THEN he acted.

The Lord will respond to you when you put him first, trust him and start moving forward. He will provide…more than you need. And he will be with you wherever you go.

Students, each of your stories should be uniquely yours. It's not about doing what everyone else is doing. It doesn't matter if you start college with your classmates. The issue is not whether you're wearing $40 underwear or grandpa's slacks. It doesn't matter if you attend college part-time. It's not important if you have a truckload of stuff for your dorm room—or only a feather duster. It doesn't matter if you work a year first, eat rice and water, commute, buy your own trombone….

But when you start the college application process, one thing *does* matter: Make sure the Lord of Financial Aid is on the case.

"I am the Lord, and there is no other." —Isaiah 45:5

Endnotes

1 Chacon, Richard. "Debt Burden Soaring for U.S. Students." *The Boston Globe.* October 23, 1997. p A1.

2 Chatzky, Jean Sherman. "So Young—and So Deep in Debt." *USA Weekend* Sunday paper magazine. March 6-8, 1998.

3 Chatzky.

4 Beddingfield, Katherine T. "Dollars for College." *The Cincinnati Post,* Oct. 19, 1994.

5 For example, Bank One's "Education One Loans." Their offer even reaches down to kindergarten, making a $60,000 maximum loan available to K-12 parents.

6 Chatzky. (for grad students it's $5800)

7 Levine, Daniel R. "The Student-Aid Swindle." *Reader's Digest.* January 1995. p. 95.

8 Ramsey, Dave. Quoted in "Author: Church Not Affecting How Members Handle Money," by Keith Todd. *Western Recorder.* Kentucky Baptist Convention. Louisville KY, February 13, 2001.

9 Burkett, Larry. *Answers to Your Family's Financial Questions.* Focus on the Family. Distributed by Tyndale House. 1987. p. 96.

10 Hurst, Blake. "My Kid's College Fund Blues." *Policy Review Magazine,* May/June 1997. Reprinted in *Reader's Digest,* November 1997.

[11] Stanley, Thomas J. "How to Live Like a Millionaire." Condensed from July 20, 1992 *Medical Economics* in *Reader's Digest*. January 1993. p. 57 ff.

[12] Belsky, Gary. "Seven Money Mistakes Everyone Makes." Condensed from July 1995 *Money* in *Reader's Digest*. January 1996.

[13] Ramsey, Dave. Quoted by Katia Hetter in "Jesus Saves, You Invest." *U.S. News and World Report*. April 27, 1998. p. 71.

[14] Hunt, Mary. "When in Doubt (Debt) Start Giving." *Focus on the Family*. May 1997. p. 10.

[15] Ramsey. ("Jesus Saves, You Invest")

[16] Ramsey. ("Author: Church Not Affecting…")

[17] Credited to Ivern Ball in *Reader's Digest*. September 1989.

[18] McCartney, Linda. Quoted by Barbara Winter. *Making a Living Without a Job*. Bantam Books. 1993. pp. 228-9.

[19] Hunt, Mary. "Dollars and Sense" column. *Homelife* magazine. LifeWay Press. Nashville TN. January 2001. p. 12.

[20] Hunt. ("Dollars and Sense")

[21] Burkett, Larry. *Your Finances in Changing Times*. Campus Crusade. 1975. p. 65.

[22] Hunt. ("Dollars and Sense")

Printed in the United States
1286500006B/550-555